MOV ELE E
ELETY

Peter Riley

W

To my granddaughter, Holly Jane.

Franklin Watts
Published in Great Britain in 2016 by The Watts Publishing Group

Text copyright © Peter Riley 2015

Editor: Hayley Fairhead
Designer: Elaine Wilkinson

ISBN: 978 1 4451 3528 1
Dewey classification number: 537

Printed in China

MIX
Paper from responsible sources
FSC
www.fsc.org
FSC® C104740

Photo acknowledgements: Baloncici/Shutterstock p4; Joe Belanger/Shutterstock p8b; Andy Crawford p19; Erika Cross/Shutterstock p5; fotorince/Shutterstock p23b; Franklin Watts p12; KPY Ivary/Shutterstock p6b; Maksim Kazakov/Shutterstock p6t; Slawomir Kruz/ Shutterstock p15b; Marbury/Shutterstock p21b, p31t; Oleksy Mark/Shutterstock front cover inset; Ray Moller p8t, p9; Sergey Nivens/Shutterstock p7, p29; Somchai Rakin/Shutterstock p10b; weerayut ranmai/Shutterstock title page, p13, p28; RoadRunnerDeLuxe/ Shutterstock p21t; Seishin 90/Dreamstime front cover main; Dmitrij Skorobogatov/ Shutterstock p20t; STILLFX/Shutterstock p20b.

All other photographs by Leon Hargreaves.
With thanks to our models Sebastian Smith-Beatty, Layomi Obanubi and Crystal Kan.

Franklin Watts
An imprint of
Hachette Children's Group
Part of The Watts Publishing Group
Carmelite House
50 Victoria Embankment
London EC4Y 0DZ

An Hachette UK Company
www.hachette.co.uk
www.franklinwatts.co.uk

All forms of electricity can be dangerous. Always treat electrical equipment with care.

Contents

Words in bold can be found in the glossary on pages 28-29.

How do we use electricity?

We use electricity every day. When we switch on a light or travel in a car we are using electricity. Some pieces of electrical equipment are called **appliances**. Electrical appliances are machines powered by electricity, which help us in many different ways.

Electricity at home

Electrical appliances give us heat to boil water, so we can cook food or warm our homes. They help move things, for example by spinning a disc in a DVD player or sending a toy car across the floor. They make things cool in a fridge, provide light in a lamp and make sound come out of a radio.

Look at the items in this kitchen. How many electrical appliances can you see?

What electrical items can you see in this city?

Using electricity outside

Electrical equipment and appliances are not just found in homes. They power streetlights, traffic lights, pedestrian crossings and automatic doors on buildings. They are found in the vehicles we use as part of the engine and in their lighting systems.

Make a list of the electrical equipment and appliances in your home. What is each item used for? Arrange them into groups according to what they do: do they give heat or light for example?

What is electricity?

Over two and a half thousand years ago in Ancient Greece, a man called Thales did an experiment. He took a piece of **amber** and rubbed it, then put it near some straw and feathers. They jumped up to the amber and stuck to it. The Greek name for amber is 'electron' and its strange power became known as electricity.

Amber is a hard yellowish solid that comes from trees that lived millions of years ago.

Static electricity

The electricity made by rubbing amber is called **static electricity**. Static electricity is a pulling force between two surfaces. You can **generate** static electricity by rubbing a dry woollen cloth on a balloon. If you press the balloon to a wall, a pulling force between the two surfaces will hold the balloon in place.

Rub a balloon against a dry cloth and hold it above some pieces of tissue paper. Static electricity pulls the paper towards the balloon.

Storm clouds

The most powerful static electricity is generated in storm clouds. Inside the cloud, water **droplets** freeze and form ice crystals and hail stones. These rub together and generate static electricity.

Electric current

In a storm, huge amounts of static electricity are released as a **current** of electricity, which flashes through the air as lightning. We use much smaller currents of electricity in our electrical equipment and appliances.

Lightning can flash from cloud to cloud or, as here, from a cloud to the ground.

You can charge a plastic pen with static electricity by rubbing it with a woollen cloth. Test the pulling force by placing the pen near small, lightweight objects and describe any changes you see.

Cells and batteries

batteries

cells

A **cell** is a store of electricity. A **battery** is a group of cells joined together. They are both used to make a current of electricity. Batteries can be used to power all sorts of things, including torches, laptop computers, mobile phones and some toys.

A cell is often shaped like a cylinder. A battery is a box in which the cells are joined together.

This car battery is made up of six cells joined together. They provide all the power for the car's engine, lights and electrical equipment, such as the radio.

Terminals of a cell

If you look closely at a cell, it has a plus sign (+) at one end and a minus sign (-) at the other end. The ends of the cells are called **terminals**. There is a positive terminal (+) and a negative terminal (-). To make electricity flow out of the cell, a **wire** must be in contact with each terminal.

Two cells are placed in a torch, with the positive terminal of one touching the negative terminal of the other.

Two cells

Sometimes two cells are joined together to make more electricity flow. They have to be joined up with the positive terminal of one cell next to the negative terminal of the other cell. If two positive terminals or two negative terminals are joined together, the electricity will not flow.

Find a toy that uses cells and take them out (you may need an adult to help you). Look for the plus and minus signs on the cells and on the inside of the toy. Can you put the cells back in correctly and make the toy work?

A bulb

Bulbs are used to provide light in the area surrounding them. Some bulbs contain a wire. When electricity passes through the wire it gets so hot that it shines and gives out light.

contacts

Bulbs used in experiments are very small and are screwed into plastic holders.

Bulbs used in science

A bulb has two places where wires are attached. They are called **contacts**. The contacts are connected to wires inside the bulb. One of the wires inside the bulb is very thin. It is in the shape of a **coil**.

The light from inside these bulbs passes through the glass and lights up the street.

Lighting a bulb

You can make a bulb light up in the following way.

1. Attach one end of a wire to one terminal of the cell.
2. Attach the other end of the wire to a contact of the bulb.
3. Attach the other terminal of the cell to the other contact of the bulb with a second wire.

Equipment:
- two wires with crocodile clips
- bulb • cell
- cell holder

The flow of electricity

Electricity flows from the cell along a wire to the bulb. When it flows through the coil of wire in the bulb, the coil gets hot and glows. The electricity continues to flow out of the bulb, along the other wire and back to the cell.

The coiled wire in a bulb gives out light, which we can see through the transparent glass that surrounds the wire.

Describe the journey of an electric current flowing along a wire from a negative terminal, through the bulb and back to the cell.

Conductors and insulators

A wire is made of metal. Electricity can flow through it. A **material** which lets electricity flow through it is called an electrical **conductor**. Some materials do not let electricity flow through them. They are called **insulators**.

What happens to the bulb when you place each of the materials in the gap in turn?

Testing conductors and insulators

You can test materials to find out if they are conductors or insulators by setting up a cell, a bulb and a gap between two wires. Place each material to be tested across the gap.

Conductors

If the material used in your experiment is a conductor, electricity will flow from the cell through the bulb, through the material in the gap and along the wire to the cell. When this happens the bulb lights up to show that the electric current is flowing. All metals conduct electricity.

Why does a cable connecting a computer to the mains have a metal wire inside and a plastic cover on the outside?

Insulators

If the material used in your experiment is an insulator, electricity cannot flow through it. It stops electricity flowing through the wires and bulb, and the bulb does not light up. Materials such as plastic, glass, paper and wood are insulators.

Mains electricity is **EXTREMELY DANGEROUS** and can harm or even kill. You must treat all electrical equipment with care.

Mains electricity is generated by power stations. The electric current flows along metal wires to people's homes.

Mains electricity

Mains electricity flows along conductors into plug sockets in your home. Insulators are used around the conductors to stop the current harming you.

A circuit

A **circuit** is the path that is set up for an electric current to flow. The parts of the circuit are called **components.**

Components of a circuit

The components of this circuit are a cell, a **switch** (see pages 18–19), a bulb and the wires that connect them up. All the components in the circuit form a loop through which the current flows.

A switch controls the flow of the current in a circuit. If the switch is on, the current flows and the bulb lights up. If the switch is off, the current does not flow.

switch

wire

Stopping the electric current

In some circuits, the switch may be on, but the bulb does not light up. This means the current is not flowing. All the components in the circuit may not be firmly connected together. A gap between any of the components or a dead cell will also stop the current flowing.

bulb

cell

Using cells, bulbs, wires and a switch, try to make your own circuit. When you have made a circuit that works, you should make a record of your experiment. You can do this by making a drawing of the components and the way they are connected together. Use the drawing of the circuit above to help you.

Trained electricians check and repair electric circuits in our homes.

A series circuit

The correct way to make a circuit is to place all the components in a line in the circuit and join them together to make a loop. This type of circuit is called a **series circuit**.

Two bulbs in a series circuit

In the circuit below there are two bulbs. They are said to be arranged in series. When two bulbs are arranged in series they do not shine as brightly as just one bulb in a circuit, because the same amount of electric current is being shared between two bulbs.

Increasing the number of bulbs in a circuit makes them shine less brightly.

Increasing the number of cells in a circuit makes the bulb shine more brightly.

Two cells in a series circuit

In this circuit two cells are arranged in series, so the negative terminal of one cell is connected by a wire to the positive terminal of the other cell. The two cells give more power to the current and the single bulb shines more brightly.

What would happen to a bulb in a circuit if you added another cell in series? What would happen if you then added another bulb in series?

Switches

Switches are used to control the flow of electricity. When you need to use an electrical appliance, such as a computer or a light, you press or click a switch and the electricity flows through it. When you have finished using the appliance you press or click again and the current stops.

The switch is off and so the bulb does not light up.

Testing a switch

You can test a switch by putting it in the gap between two wires that are connected to a cell and a bulb. When the switch is on, the electric current flows and the bulb lights up. When the switch is off, the electric current does not flow and the bulb does not light up.

Make your own simple switch

Loop your paper clip under one drawing pin. Push the drawing pins into the wood so that the paper clip can touch both pins. Connect the wires to the pins using the crocodile clips. The paper clip now acts as a switch and is ready to use.

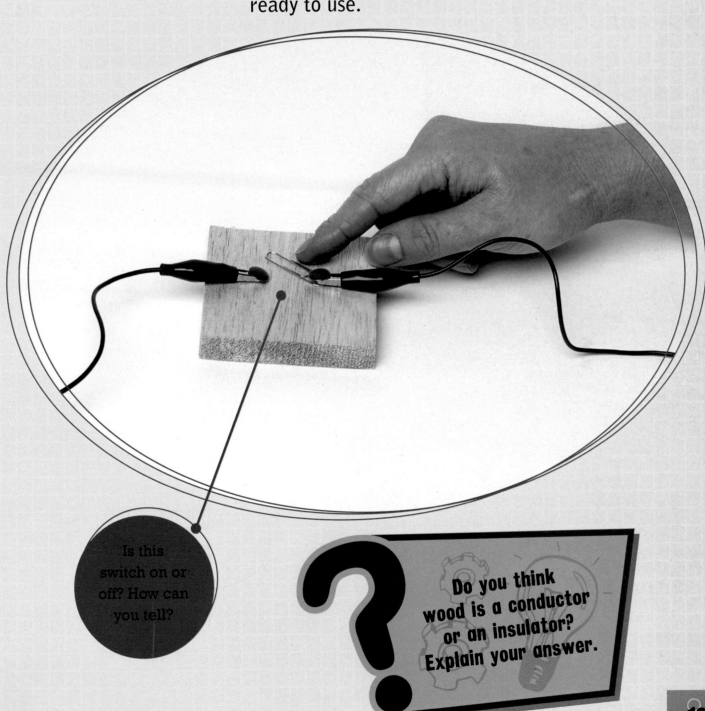

Is this switch on or off? How can you tell?

Do you think wood is a conductor or an insulator? Explain your answer.

Voltage

The power of a cell is called its **voltage** and is measured in units called **volts**. The symbol for this unit is V. You can see the voltage written on the side of the cell.

These cells each have a voltage of 1.2V.

Increasing the voltage

When two cells are joined together, the power of one cell is added to the power of the other. If two 1.5V cells are joined together correctly in a circuit they give a power of 3V (1.5 + 1.5 = 3V). A battery can have a number of cells joined together inside it. This makes the battery more powerful than a single cell. Some batteries have a voltage of 4.5V, 6V or even 9V.

This 6V battery is used in large torches to provide a wide beam of light, or in a lantern where the bulb shines in all directions.

Voltage of a bulb

Bulbs are made to work at certain voltages such as up to 1.5V, up to 4.5V and up to 6V. If a bulb is put in a circuit where the cells supply a higher voltage, the coil of wire in the bulb gets so hot it melts and breaks, and the current stops flowing.

When the coil of wire in a bulb breaks, we say the bulb has burnt out.

If one fairy light burns out, all the lights will go out if they are connected in series.

1. How many 1.5V cells are in a 4.5V battery?
2. Will a 1.5V bulb work with a 1.5V cell in the circuit?
3. Will a 3.5V bulb work with two 1.5V cells in the circuit?

Buzzer and motor

Buzzers and motors can be found in many electrical appliances. Buzzers can be used in burglar alarms. A buzzer makes a sound when electricity passes through it. Motors can be used in fans. An electric motor has a **shaft**. Electricity passes through the electric motor, which spins the shaft.

The parts that produce the buzzing sound in a buzzer are delicate. They are protected by a plastic case.

A buzzer in a series circuit

A buzzer is designed to work up to a certain voltage. There is a label on the buzzer to show this voltage. A buzzer has a red wire and a black wire. It must be placed in the circuit carefully. The red wire must be attached to a wire coming from the positive terminal of the cell. The black wire must be attached to the wire coming from the negative terminal of the cell. If the wires are the wrong way round, the buzzer will not work.

cell

buzzer

A motor in a series circuit

A motor is designed to work up to a certain voltage. There are two contacts on the motor where wires can be attached. The wires do not have to be attached in a special way, unlike the wires of the buzzer.

cell

motor

The motor shaft sticks out of a metal case. If you attach an object to it, the shaft will make the object spin around.

A motor spins this fan, which moves the surrounding air to produce a cooling breeze.

Look around your home for electrical appliances that turn things (but do not switch them on). Each one will have an electric motor. How many can you find? What does each appliance do?

A lighthouse

Electric circuits can be used to make models. You can make a model lighthouse for example, using a simple circuit.

Building your lighthouse

1.
The main part of the lighthouse is made from a plastic bottle. Attach the bulb to the top of the bottle with some adhesive tack.

2.
Take the strip of thick card and bring the two ends together to make a circle. Stick the ends together with sticky tape and place this over the top of the bottle so that it rests on top. Cut windows in each side of the small box and stick this to the circle of card to make your lantern room.

3.
Connect the wires to the bulb and stick these to the sides of the bottle with sticky tape. Add the cell and switch to complete the series circuit. The wires could be covered with paper to hide them.

4.
A lighthouse flashes light in a certain way, such as three flashes every 30 seconds. You could use a stopwatch to time the flashes on your model lighthouse by switching the light on and off every few seconds.

Robot head

You can make a robot head with two simple circuits. Make your robot's eyes light up – he can buzz too!

1.
Create a circuit with the two bulbs, a switch and a cell. Cut two eye holes into the cardboard box and stick the bulbs inside them using sticky tape. Cut a nose hole and stick the switch inside it. Cut a mouth hole and stick the cell inside it.

2.
When you tweak the robot's nose, you switch on the circuit and its eyes light up.

3.
To make your robot buzz when you pat his head, you will need another circuit and a homemade switch. Make the switch by folding a piece of cardboard and sticking two pieces of aluminium foil inside. Attach a wire to each piece of foil. Complete the circuit with a cell and a buzzer.

4.
Attach the switch to the top of the robot's head with sticky tape. When you pat the robot's head it buzzes!

What would happen if an extra cell was added to both of the circuits in the robot's head?

Glossary

Adhesive tack a sticky substance used to join items together.

Amber a honey-coloured solid formed from the hardened juice made by trees that lived millions of years ago.

Appliance a machine powered by electricity that helps us, for example, a washing machine or tumble dryer.

Battery two or more cells joined together in a line. The positive terminal of one cell is connected to the negative terminal of the next.

Bulb a component in a circuit that gives out light when a current of electricity passes through it.

Cell a store of electricity. It contains substances that make a current flow round a circuit when the circuit is switched on.

Circuit an arrangement of electrical components looped together so that when they are all connected together electricity flows.

Coil a length of wire that has been curled round into a row of circular loops.

Components the pieces of equipment that make up parts of a circuit, such as wires, bulbs and cells.

Conductor a material that allows a current of electricity to pass through it.

Contact a place on an electrical component where a wire is attached to make part of a circuit.

Current the flow of electricity.

Droplets a very tiny drop.

Generate to make electricity by rubbing a balloon on wool. Substances in a cell generate electricity when a circuit is switched on.

Insulator a material that does not allow a current of electricity to pass through it. Plastic is an insulator.

Material anything that contains matter in one of its three states – solid, liquid or gas.

Series circuit a circuit in which all the components form a line.

Shaft the section or part driven round by a motor.

Static electricity a form of electricity made by rubbing. Static electricity does not flow or move like an electric current.

Switch a component that controls the flow of electric current by letting it flow or stopping it flowing in a circuit.

Terminal the part of a cell which is attached to a wire in a circuit. Electricity flows from the negative terminal to the positive terminal.

Volt a unit that measures the power of electricity.

Voltage a measure of the power of a cell in volts.

Wire a long thin strand of metal that conducts electricity. Wires are usually covered in plastic.

Answers to the activities and questions

Page 5 How do we use electricity?

Activity: This will vary with each home. Examples are a kettle, iron or hairdryer to provide heat; lamps to provide light; a motor in a food processor to mash up food.

Page 7 What is electricity?

Activity: A plastic pen should be rubbed with a dry woollen cloth about ten or more times and brought very close (without touching) to some torn-up tiny pieces of paper. The tiny pieces of paper will jump towards the pen.

Page 9 Cells and batteries

Activity: The toy should work when it is switched on. This shows that the cells are arranged correctly and have a store of electricity. As they are removed, the + and - signs on the cells and inside the toy should be looked for so they can be matched when the cells are returned. The cells are usually held in with springs to make sure they make firm contact with the wires in the circuit.

Page 11 A bulb

Activity: An electric current flows from the negative terminal along the wire to the bulb. As the current flows through the bulb, it heats up the coil and makes it shine and give out light. The current then flows along the next wire to the positive terminal of the cell.

Page 13 Conductors and insulators

Answer: The metal wire is a conductor of electricity and lets the electric current flow to the computer. The plastic in the coating is an insulator and stops the current of electricity from leaving the sides of the wire.

Page 15 A circuit

Here are some examples of circuits you could draw:

Page 17 A series circuit

Answer: It would get brighter. The bulbs would get dimmer.

Page 19 Switches

Answer: The switch is off because the paper clip is not touching the other drawing pin. Wood is an insulator. If it was a conductor, the current of the electricity would pass from one drawing pin to the other when the switch was off and the current would flow all the time.

Page 21 Voltage

Answers: 1. Three 2. Yes 3. Yes

Page 23 Buzzer and motor

Activity: Motors can be found in microwaves to make the turntable spin or in DVD players to make a DVD spin.

Page 27 Robot head

Activity: Care must be taken to keep the two circuits separate in the model. If two cells are added to each circuit, the eyes shine more brightly and the robot buzzes more loudly.

Index

About this book

Moving Up with Science is designed to help children develop the following skills:

Science enquiry skills: researching using secondary sources, all pages; grouping and classifying pages 5 and 23; comparative test, page 12.

Working scientifically skills: making careful observations, pages 7, 9 and 23; setting up a practical enquiry, pages 7, 11, 25 and 27; make comparative tests, page 12; using results to draw simple conclusions, page 7; using straightforward scientific evidence to answer questions, page 12.

Critical thinking skills: knowledge, all pages; comprehension, pages 13, 17, 21 and 27; analysis, page 19.